Young Champions: It's All About Attitude

Linda Barr
AR B.L.: 3.2
Points: 0.5   MG

Young Champions

It's All About Attitude

Linda Barr

Reading Consultant:
Timothy Rasinski, Ph.D.
Professor of Reading Education
Kent State University

Content Consultant:
Maria Portgee
Communication and Development Manager
U.S. Disabled Athletes Fund/BlazeSports America

Red Brick™ Learning

Published by Red Brick™ Learning
7825 Telegraph Road, Bloomington, Minnesota 55438
http://www.redbricklearning.com

Library of Congress Cataloging-in-Publication Data
Barr, Linda, 1944–
  Young champions: it's all about attitude / by Linda Barr; reading
  consultant, Timothy Rasinski.
    p. cm.—(High five reading)
  Includes bibliographical references and index.
    ISBN 0-7368-5742-7 (soft cover)—ISBN 0-7368-5732-X (hard cover)
    1. Athletes with disabilities—United States—Biography. I. Rasinski,
Timothy V. II. Title. III. Series.
GV697.A1B39 2006
796'.092'2—dc22

                                                        2005010021

Created by Kent Publishing Services, Inc.
Designed by Signature Design Group, Inc.
Edited by Jerry Ruff, Managing Editor, Red Brick™ Learning
Red Brick™ Learning Editorial Director: Mary Lindeen

This publisher has made every effort to trace ownership of all copyrighted
material and to secure necessary permissions. In the event of any questions
arising as to the use of any material, the publisher, while expressing regret for
any inadvertent error, will be happy to make necessary corrections.

Photo Credits:
Cover, pages 18, 21, 23, courtesy of Lisa Franks; pages 4, 7, Jane Hale,
Associated Press, A/P; page 9, Nevins/A-Frame, Zuma Press; page 11,
D. Fujimoto/The Garden Island, Zuma Press; page 12, Michael Germana, UPI
Photo Service; pages 15, 17, courtesy of Jake Porter; page 25, Rick Hickman,
Lake Charles American Press, Associated Press, A/P; pages 26, 27, 29, Mohave
Valley Daily News, Associated Press, A/P; page 31, J.D. Pooley, Sentinal-Tribune,
Associated Press, A/P; page 32, Mark Cowan, Icon SMI; pages 34, 37, Kelly
LaDuke; page 39, Associated Press, A/P; page 41, Carlos Diaz/INFGoff.com,
Showcase; page 43, Fayez Nureldine, Agence France Presse

Printed in the United States of America.

1 2 3 4 5 6 11 10 09 08 07 06 05

Table of Contents

*Willie McQueen plays high school football
for Flint Southwest Academy.*

CHAPTER 1

Courage

*You do not have to win to be a **champion**.*

*You just need to face your **challenges**.*

In this book, you will meet eight champions.

Each one faces special challenges.

All share something called courage.

Willie and the Train

Willie McQueen was playing with his cousins by railroad tracks. Willie was only 7. A train came and Willie tried to go under it. The train dragged him 50 yards (46 meters). It cut off Willie's legs at the hip.

---

champion (CHAM-pee-uhn): a fighter; someone who battles bravely

challenge (CHAL-uhnj): something that is hard and takes extra work to do

"I Know Who I Am"

Willie was lucky to live. Still, he was badly hurt. Many people would have given up. Willie did not. In fact, Willie plays **defensive tackle** for his high school. On the football field, he moves by pushing off the ground with his arms.

Willie is very strong and quick. "When Willie gets his hands on you, you are going down," one of his coaches said about him.

Willie says, "I don't feel sorry for myself. I know who I am. I know what I can do." His courage makes his team work harder.

Willie lost both legs. But he still plays football. He still goes to high school. He has a full life. So does the surfer you will meet next.

---

defensive tackle (di-FEN-siv TAK-uhl): a player who tries to stop the other team from moving the ball forward

Willie likes math. He hopes to start his own business someday.

Swimming with Sharks

Imagine that a shark bit off your arm.
Would you ever go back into the ocean?
Bethany Hamilton did. She has courage.

Bethany lives in Hawaii. She is a surfer.
At age 11, she began to **compete** at surfing.
By age 13, she was a **respected** surfer.
One day, she was surfing for fun when a
14-foot (4.3-meter) shark attacked her.
Bethany lost her arm.

When the shark bit, Bethany stayed cool.
"I wasn't that scared," she said later.
Ten weeks later, she was surfing again.
Ten months later, she won a surfing contest.
She also made the National Surfing Team.

---

compete (kuhm-PEET): to enter contests
respected (ri-SPEKT-ed): admired

Bethany lost her arm in a shark attack.
That did not stop her from surfing.

Becoming Stronger

Bethany's life changed when she lost her arm. But she also became stronger. She wants to help others become stronger. Bethany has written a book about it. Soon there will be a movie about Bethany.

Bethany will keep surfing. She will also keep winning. She does not need two arms. She just needs courage. Bethany has plenty of that.

Bethany and Willie McQueen both have something else, too. They have **confidence**. They know what they can do, and they do it!

---

confidence (KON-fuh-dehns): knowing that you can do something

Fireman Tim Terrazas shows the bite mark in
Bethany's surfboard.

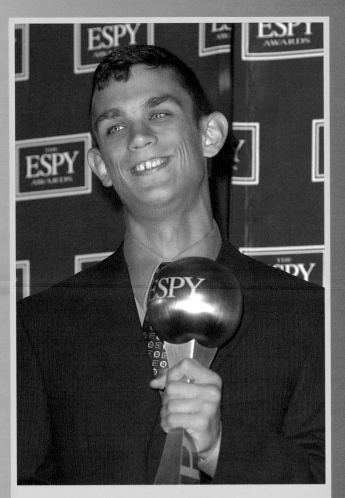

"No one will remember the score 20 years
from now, but they will remember what
Jake Porter did," said his coach.
In 2003, Jake received the ESPY Award.
The award is for the best sports moment of the year.

CHAPTER 2

Confidence

Sometimes it is hard to feel good about yourself.
It can be even harder if you have trouble learning.
Still, with confidence, you can do many things.
You can even score touchdowns!

Football Player

Jake Porter has **Fragile-X Syndrome**. Jake was born with this condition that makes it hard for him to learn and do things. Still, Jake played football at his high school. Jake went to Northwest High School in McDermott, Ohio.

Fragile-X Syndrome (FRAJ-il-EKS SIN-drohm): a condition that makes it hard to learn and do some things

A Game to Remember

Jake practiced every day with the team. Mostly, he sat on the bench during games. Jake's coach wanted to let him catch the ball at one game.

Finally, Jake got his chance. His team was playing against Waverly High School. The coaches of both teams agreed to let Jake catch a ball at the end of the game.

By the end of the game, Jake's team was losing 42-0. But Waverly decided that Jake mattered more than a **shutout**.

Jake's team passed him the ball. Jake made the catch. He began to run. No one tried to stop him. Both teams cheered. So did the fans. Jake scored a touchdown!

---

shutout (SHUHT-out): a game in which one team scores no points

Jake ran 49 yards for his touchdown.

Did You See Jake?

Jake's touchdown was shown on TV. Millions of people watched him run. Soon the whole nation knew about him.

People were proud of Jake. They were also proud of both coaches and their teams. Jake's mom said, "We sometimes forget what's really important." But these two teams remembered.

Jake has confidence. He knows that he has something to give. His **outlook** gives others confidence. Jake wants to make the most of his life. And he does it every day!

---

outlook (OUT-luk): a way of looking at things

Jake does work for the principal of his school. Jake does his job and everything with joy. He inspires other students at his school.

*An illness paralyzed Lisa Franks.
That did not stop her from being a top athlete.*

CHAPTER 3

Outlook

Imagine you can't use your legs! What will you do?

Some young people cannot walk, but they can race!

In this chapter, you will meet two of these people.

Lisa and Michael make the most of their lives!

They have a positive outlook.

Lisa Franks

Lisa Franks has always been an **athlete**. She helped her high school basketball team become the city champs.

Soon after that, Lisa got sick. First, she could not stand up. Then, she could not move her arms. She was **paralyzed**.

---

athlete (ATH-leet): a person who is trained in or very good at a sport
paralyze (PAR-uh-lize): to make unable to move

Fighting Back

At first, Lisa felt sorry for herself. She asked, "Why did this happen to me?" Then she changed her outlook. She decided to do something with her life.

Lisa began to **exercise**. She wanted to use her arms again. Slowly they got stronger. She learned to feed herself. She began to push herself in her wheelchair. She learned to dress herself.

Then, Lisa's life changed again. She learned about wheelchair sports. Soon, she was racing!

---

exercise (EK-sur-size): to make your body work hard in order to keep fit and healthy

The first wheelchair sport Lisa tried was rugby. Later she tried wheelchair racing.

Confined? Not Lisa!

Lisa has won races all around the world. She has many medals. Most of them are gold medals. She has also set many records. Several groups have named her **Female** Athlete of the Year.

Lisa does well because of her positive outlook. She knows she is not **confined** to her wheelchair. She knows she is free to do her best.

Lisa goes to college now. She wants to be an **engineer**. Nothing seems to stop her.

Like Lisa, Michael Timpa cannot walk. Still, he can race, too! He also has the right outlook.

---

female (FEE-male): a girl or woman
confine (kuhn-FINE): to keep in one place
engineer (en-juh-NIHR): someone who plans how to build things

Lisa raced for Canada in the 2002 World Championships in France. She won four gold medals.

The Winner!

Michael Timpa is from Louisiana.
He was born with a problem in his **spine**.
He cannot walk. Michael has used a
wheelchair his entire life.

Still, Michael is faster than most people.
He can push his wheelchair nearly one-half
mile (805 meters) in less than two minutes!
Michael was the best high school wheelchair
racer in the United States.

Michael, Lisa, and the other young people
in this book are the same in many ways.
They have a positive outlook. They also
have something called **determination**.
Do you know what determination means?

---

spine (SPINE): a long row of connected bones that form
the backbone
determination (di-TUR-min-AY-shuhn): wanting to do
something very badly

In 2004, Michael was the National Wheelchair Athlete of the Year.

Teammates use sign language to talk with Amanda Andrews (right).

Chapter 4

Determination

Most people have goals. Think about your own goals.

What are they? Will your goals be hard to reach?

Sometimes reaching goals takes great determination.

Amanda and Allison have plenty of that.

Talking with Her Hands

Amanda Andrews loves basketball. She plays on her high school team.

Amanda can hear only very loud sounds. For example, she cannot hear people talking. She was born with this hearing loss. Amanda uses sign language to talk. Her finger movements stand for words.

Using Eyes, Not Ears

Amanda cannot hear her coach. She cannot hear her teammates. She cannot hear a whistle blow. Still, she is determined to play.

Johnny Cox helps Amanda. He is an **interpreter**. First, he listens to the coach. Then he uses sign language to tell Amanda what the coach said.

The coach is learning sign language, too. She uses it with the whole team. Then she can "talk" to them even when the crowd is very loud.

Amanda's coach said that nothing stops Amanda. Amanda has determination. Let's meet another young woman who knows something about determination.

---

interpreter (in-TUR-prit-uhr): a person who puts speech into a different language for someone else to understand

Amanda's coach (woman in white shirt, center) talks to the team. Amanda is on the left. She is watching Johnny Cox (in sweatshirt). Cox is using sign language to tell her what the coach is saying.

Taking a Chance

Allison Ahlfeldt (ALL-felt) is from California. She was born without her lower right leg. Still, she was determined to walk. Allison chose to wear a **prosthetic** leg. Now she walks where she wants!

Allison loves volleyball. She began to play in fifth grade. At age 21, she took a chance. She tried out for the U.S. Volleyball **Disabled** Team.

Here's the surprise. The rest of the players were men! But Allison still made the team. She was their first female player!

Allison always finds a way to play the sport she loves.

prosthetic (pross-THEH-tik): not real; substitute
disabled (diss-AY-buhld): limited in what you can do

30

Was That Fair?

In 1998, Allison's team went to Poland. There, the **international** volleyball group would not let Allison play. She had to sit on the bench. Her missing leg was not the problem. She could not play because she is a woman!

Allison knows the rules will change someday. She is still determined to play.

---

international (in-tur-NASH-uh-nuhl): having to do with several countries

Allison plays on the USA Women's National Sitting Volleyball Team.

A New Team

Now Allison has joined a new team. She is a top player on that team, too!

Allison plays for the USA Women's National Sitting Volleyball Team. All members of her team have a disability to their lower body.

Allison has to be strong to be such a good volleyball player. Next, you will meet Kyle Maynard. In Kyle's sport, strength is even more important. But Kyle—like all the champions in this book—is strong in more ways than one.

Kyle Maynard wrestles young men who have much longer arms and legs. He usually wins.

CHAPTER 5

Strength

What is strength? Is it how much you can lift?

Is it how many push-ups or sit-ups you can do?

Kyle Maynard is much stronger than most people.

Kyle's greatest strength is his heart!

Kyle Maynard, Champion

Kyle Maynard says, "It's not what I can do. It's what I WILL do." Anyone can say that. Kyle means it.

This young man is a top **wrestler**. Kyle was born with very short arms and legs. He is less than 3 feet (1 meter) tall.

---

wrestler (RESS-luhr): an athlete who tries to throw or force an opponent to the ground

Growing Up Tough

Kyle's parents did not baby him. He learned to feed himself because his father **insisted**.

Kyle holds the spoon between the ends of his arms. He scoops up food. Then he turns the spoon around and puts it in his mouth.

Even without fingers, Kyle has perfect handwriting. He can even type 50 words a minute!

This young man never says, "I can't." In middle school, he played football. He wore socks and pads on his small feet. The other players wore **cleats**.

---

insist (in-SIST): to demand that someone do something
cleats (KLEETZ): metal pieces on the bottom of shoes that dig into the grass

Kyle has three younger sisters. He used to play hide-and-seek and have water fights with them. They still wrestle together, but Kyle lets them win.

Reaching the Top

Kyle worked hard to become a wrestler. For the first two years, he lost every **match**. Still, he did not give up. Finally, Kyle and his coach tried some new **holds** using his chin and arms. Kyle started to win.

In his final year of high school, Kyle made the wrestling team. Then he became one of the top wrestlers in his state.

In high school, Kyle also belonged to many clubs. He swam and played baseball. He got mostly A's in his classes.

---

match (MACH): a contest
hold (HOHLD): a way to grab onto a person in wrestling

Kyle works out with weights to build his strength.

Looking Ahead

Kyle goes to college now. He still wrestles.
He also speaks to many groups.

"Anyone can overcome their **boundaries**,"
Kyle says. He helps people change their lives.
He gets them to look at their strengths.
He urges them to think about what they
can do—and what they WILL do.

Champions All

There are many types of champions.
What makes someone a champion, though?
Is it courage and confidence? How about
outlook? Maybe strength and determination?
Or is it all of these? Which of these **qualities**
do you have? Which ones WILL you have?

---

boundary (BOUN-duh-ree): a limit
quality (KWAHL-uh-tee): a special characteristic or
feature of someone

*Kyle urges people to look at their strengths.
"Anyone can overcome their boundaries," he says.*

Epilogue

Paralympic Games

The Paralympic Games are held after each Olympics. More than 5,000 top athletes with physical disabilities compete in the games. These men and women come from 120 countries.

The athletes in these games all have some kind of challenge. Some are blind. Some were injured. Some were born without an arm or a leg.

These athletes play 21 sports. They all have courage and confidence. They all have determination and strength. They all have a positive outlook. They all **inspire** others to do their very best.

---

inspire (in-SPIRE): to give someone courage or hope

Athletes at the Paralympics can do many things—and do them well!

Glossary

athlete (ATH-leet): a person who is trained in or very good at a sport

boundary (BOUN-duh-ree): a limit

challenge (CHAL-uhnj): something that is hard and takes extra work to do

champion (CHAM-pee-uhn): a fighter; someone who battles bravely

cleats (KLEETZ): metal pieces on the bottom of shoes that dig into the grass

compete (kuhm-PEET): to enter contests

confidence (KON-fuh-dehns): knowing that you can do something

confine (kuhn-FINE): to keep in one place

defensive tackle (di-FEN-siv TAK-uhl): a player who tries to stop the other team from moving the ball forward

determination (di-TUR-min-AY-shuhn): wanting to do something very badly

disabled (diss-AY-buhld): limited in what you can do

engineer (en-juh-NIHR): someone who plans how to build things

exercise (EK-sur-size): to make your body work hard in order to keep fit and healthy

female (FEE-male): a girl or woman

Fragile-X Syndrome (FRAJ-il-EKS SIN-drohm): a condition that makes it hard to learn and do some things

hold (HOHLD): a way to grab onto a person in wrestling

insist (in-SIST): to demand that someone do something

inspire (in-SPIRE): to give someone courage or hope

international (in-tur-NASH-uh-nuhl): having to do with several countries

interpreter (in-TUR-prit-uhr): a person who puts speech into a different language for someone else to understand

match (MACH): a contest

outlook (OUT-luk): a way of looking at things

paralyze (PAR-uh-lize): to make unable to move

prosthetic (pross-THEH-tik): not real; substitute

quality (KWAHL-uh-tee): a special characteristic or feature of someone

respected (ri-SPEKT-ed): admired

shutout (SHUHT-out): a game in which one team scores no points

spine (SPINE): a long row of connected bones that form the backbone

wrestler (RESS-luhr): an athlete who tries to throw or force an opponent to the ground

Bibliography

Brown, Fern. *Special Olympics.* A First Book. New York: Franklin Watts, 1992.

Dinn, Sheila. *Hearts of Gold: A Celebration of Special Olympics and Its Heroes.* Woodbridge, Conn.: Blackbirch Press, 1996.

Hamilton, Bethany. *Soul Surfer: A True Story of Faith, Family, and Fighting to Get Back on the Board.* New York: Pocketbooks, MTV Books, 2004.

Kennedy, Mike. *Special Olympics.* A True Book. New York: Children's Press, 2003.

Useful Addresses

Disabled Sports USA
451 Hungerford Drive, Suite 100
Rockville, MD 20850

Special Olympics
1133 19th Street NW
Washington, D.C. 20036

U.S. Disabled Athletes Fund
280 Interstate North Circle, Suite 450
Atlanta, GA 30339

U.S. Paralympics
One Olympic Plaza
Colorado Springs, CO 80909

Internet Sites

BlazeSports America/U.S. Disabled Athletes Fund
http://www.blazesports.com

Special Olympics
http://www.specialolympics.org

U.S. Paralympics
http://www.usparalympics.org

Index